Mathstraks 10-11
Activities for Better Numeracy
Lesley Higgin

Publisher's Note

Lesley Higgin's tried and tested activities in this volume will enliven hundreds of classrooms and homework sessions across the world.

An experienced teacher and author, she brings practicality and a sense of fun to what can often seem dull learning and reinforcement tasks.

Junior Mathstraks are available in book and ebook form covering ages 7-8, 8-9, 9-10 and Extension for ages 11 and above - as well as this volume.

In addition there are Mathstraks volumes for early Secondary years on Algebra, Geometry and Number.

You can keep up to date with this and other new titles, special offers and more, through registering on our website for our e-mail newsletter or following us on Twitter or Facebook.

Published by Tarquin Publications
Suite 74, 17 Holywell Hill
St Albans
AL1 1DT

www.tarquingroup.com

Distributed in the USA by Parkwest
www.parkwestpubs.com
www.amazon.com & major retailers

Distributed in Australia by OLM www.lat-olm.com.au

Copyright © Lesley Higgin, 2016
ISBN: 978-1-907-55079-9
Ebook ISBN: 978-1-911-09329-9

Printed and designed in the United Kingdom

Intoduction

It's always a challenge to be able to provide enough opportunity for children to practise number work, without them getting bored with repetitive exercises. I hope that this book will help.

I have developed the *Mathstraks* series to enable pupils to gain a solid understanding of numeracy through fun, challenge and play.

There are lots of different activities to enable children to use their number skills in a variety of situations, including puzzles, problem-solving and games. I have enjoyed writing the tasks and they have worked extremely well with my classes.

I hope you find the book useful and, most importantly, that the children enjoy it.

Lesley Higgin

Make 10

Cut out the following squares

Match them so that each pair of adjacent sides add to 10.

	5.98			2.07			7.46	
7.5	A	7.7	6.1	B	0.01	9.09	C	4.09
	0.7			4.2			1.7	
	7.55			8.93			9.03	
2.3	D	3.09	8.5	E	0.91	9.9	F	3.9
	1.07			0.07			2.45	
	2.55			9.3			5.8	
9.5	G	0.1	2.03	H	1.5	6.91	I	3.99
	4.02			5.2			2.54	

Decimal Addition Grids

A

+				
0.3	1			
		1		0.8
	1.2		0.6	
		1.7	1	

B

+				
	1		1.21	
		1.24	1	
		1		0.91
0.26				1

Challenge

Put the numbers 0.4, 0.5, 0.6, 0.7, 0.8 and 0.9 in the shaded boxes:

+			
		1	1.5
	1.3	0.9	

(handwritten top right: 3.09 − 2.18 = .91)

Till Trouble

The till at the '*Fresh 4 U*' is broken and often misses sections of print.

Calculate and fill in the missing amounts on the following receipts:

(handwritten: 1.20 + 0.99 = 3.09 ✓, 2.19 2.18 ✓, 0.91)

Receipt 1

Fresh 4 U	
1kg apples	£1.20
1 mango	£0.99
1 punnet strawberries	£0.91
total	£3.09

Receipt 2

Fresh 4 U	
2kg apples	£
1kg oranges	£1.49
1 punnet blueberries	£1.50
total	£

Receipt 3

Fresh 4 U	
5kg potatoes	£2.50
1 lemon	£
2 punnets blueberries	£
total	£5.65

Receipt 4

Fresh 4 U	
2kg potatoes	£
2 mangoes	£
3 lemons	£
total	£

Receipt 5

Fresh 4 U	
2kg oranges	£
1 banana	£
3kg apples	£
total	£6.78

Receipt 6

Fresh 4 U	
7 bananas	£
3 mangoes	£
1kg pears	£
total	£5.42

Receipt 7

Fresh 4 U	
1 bag mushrooms	£
2kg pears	£
3 bananas	£
total	£3.65

Receipt 8

Fresh 4 U	
2 bags mushrooms	£
½ kg apples	£
5 lemons	£
total	£

Receipt 9

Fresh 4 U	
3 punnets strawberries	£
1½ kg apples	£
2½ kg potatoes	£
total	£

Challenge!

1. Joe spent £10 exactly at '*Fresh 4 U*'. What might he have bought?

2. Sarah paid with a £10 note and got £5.40 change. What might she have bought?

Right Height

All the children in a village have their heights measured. Use the clues to match each child with their height and write their names above.

1.2m	1.01m	0.75m	1.08m
1.74m	1.26m	1.55m	0.95m
0.8m	1.3m	0.91m	1.16m
1.38m	1.12m	1.5m	1.27m

- William is the shortest child.
- Tina is the tallest.
- George is twice as tall as William.
- Harriet is 1cm taller than Robin.
- Olga is 10cm shorter than Robin.
- Hannah is 19cm shorter than Tina.
- Hannah is the same height as William and Harry together.
- Ursula is taller than Olga, but shorter than Robin.
- Alice and Tom are both under a metre tall.
- Tom is taller than Alice.
- Isobel is 10cm taller than Alice.
- Sam is 33cm taller than the shortest child.
- Yvette is taller than Sam, but shorter than Olga.
- Isaac is 8cm taller than Emma.

Challenge!

Write out the names of the children in height order from shortest to tallest. The first letters of the names should spell out a question for you to answer.

Negative Arrows

Move around the following grids, filling in the answers as you go.

A. When you move right subtract 2. When you move up subtract 1

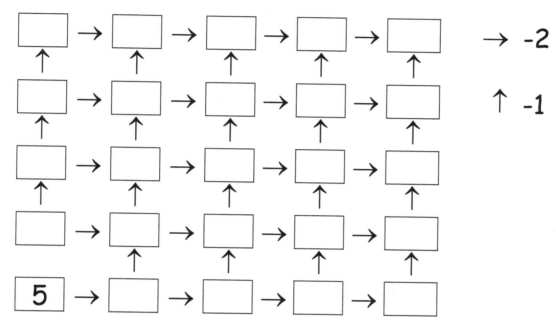

B. When you move right subtract 10. When you move up subtract 6

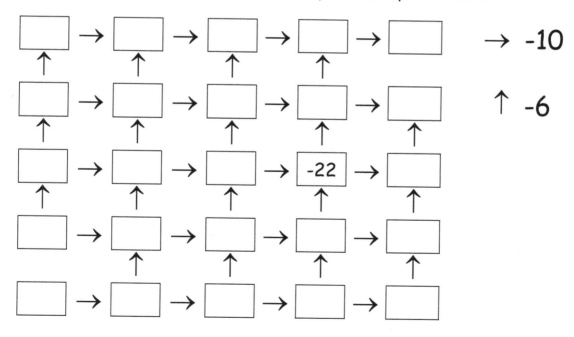

The Weather Report

A weather reporter gives details of temperatures in various cities around the world on a particular day.

Use the clues to work out which city has which temperature.

City	Temp	City	Temp
_____	-12°C	_____	4 °C
_____	15 °C	_____	25 °C
_____	-2 °C	_____	1 °C
_____	-4 °C	_____	-20 °C
_____	26 °C	_____	-5 °C
_____	18 °C	_____	-3 °C
_____	-10 °C	_____	-7 °C

- The coldest city was Helsinki.
- The warmest city was Sydney.
- Reykjavic was 16 °C warmer than Helsinki.
- London was 28 °C colder than Sydney.
- Oslo was 3 °C colder than Reykjavic.
- Paris was 3 °C warmer than London.
- Moscow was 10 °C warmer than Helsinki.
- Delhi was 20 °C warmer than London.
- Vienna was 21 °C colder than Delhi.
- Venice was 11 °C warmer than Oslo.
- Calgary was 2 °C colder than Moscow.
- Tunis was 18 °C warmer than Vienna.
- Cape Town was 30 °C warmer than Edinburgh.

Now write out all the cities in ascending order of temperature.

Sums and Differences for Negative Numbers

Work out the missing numbers in the following grids like this:

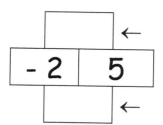

The sum of the two numbers goes here (3)

The difference of the two numbers goes here (7)

You might find it helpful to draw a number line.
Remember that a difference is always positive.

1.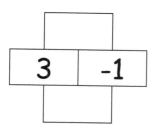

2.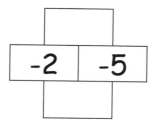

3.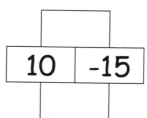

4.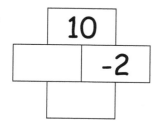

5.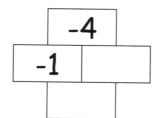

6.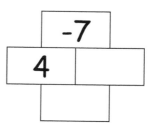

In questions 7, 8 and 9 find <u>two</u> possible ways of completing each grid:

7.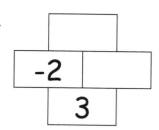

8.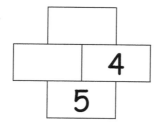

9.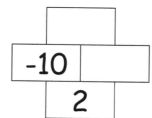

Dice Digits

- Throw 2 dice (1 to 6) and make a two digit number to fit one of the following definitions. For example, if you throw a 1 and a 6, you could make 16 or 61.

- You may only choose one number and one corresponding definition per turn.

- Fill in your numbers as you play.

- The winner is the first person to have a correct number in each category.

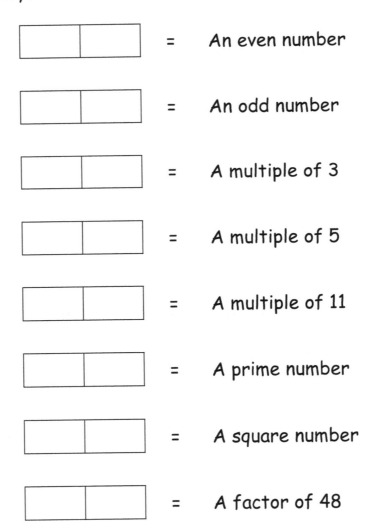

	=	An even number
	=	An odd number
	=	A multiple of 3
	=	A multiple of 5
	=	A multiple of 11
	=	A prime number
	=	A square number
	=	A factor of 48

Make a Multiplication

A. Use the numbers 3, 4, 5 once each in the following spaces to make the different types of number listed below.

$$\boxed{} \times \boxed{\,\vert\,}$$

In each case make a note of how you arrange the numbers and your solution.

1. An even number.
2. An odd number.
3. A number ending in 0.
4. The greatest possible number.

B. Now use the numbers 2, 3, 4, 5 once each in the following spaces:

$$\boxed{\,\vert\,} \times \boxed{\,\vert\,}$$

1. An odd number.
2. A number ending in zero.
3. A number greater than 2000.
4. The smallest possible number.

C. Now use the numbers 1, 2, 3, 4, 5 once each in the following spaces:

$$\boxed{\,\vert\,} \times \boxed{\,\vert\,\,\vert\,}$$

1. An even number
2. A number ending in 5.
3. A number greater than 22000.

Challenge!

In part C, what is the smallest possible number you can make?

Student Sheet

Make 120

On the following grid, try to find lines of 2, 3, 4 or 5 numbers which multiply to make 120.

The lines may be horizontal, vertical or diagonal.

Draw a line through each group you find.

2	11	3	2	2	14	7	2	6	5	13	11	2	9	2	3	2	10
2	3	9	13	7	3	9	12	9	7	2	14	3	2	2	9	13	11
15	20	14	3	10	20	13	5	4	3	7	8	4	13	3	5	4	2
2	10	3	2	11	6	12	2	3	11	13	9	30	15	2	7	13	10
9	13	2	7	2	13	9	3	2	2	2	14	2	11	9	5	2	6

What is the answer?

Challenge!

How many different pairs of whole numbers can you find which multiply to make 120?

What is the largest group of whole numbers (excluding 1), which will multiply to make 120?

Number Names

Codes are used in lots of situations, but especially in computers. When you send information over the internet, it is coded so that only the recipient can read the information.

A simple way of coding is to give letters numbers. You can give a word or name a code by multiplying the value of the letters.

For example, if D = 4, A = 1 and N = 14, then the name DAN could have a code of 56.

Using A=1, B=2, C=3, D=4............solve the following coding questions:

A. Work out the codes for these names:

1. JO   2. JOE   3. LARA   4. MAX

5. PAM   6. LEE   7. DIANA   8. ZOE

B. Work out possible names for these codes:

	Code	Name
1.	260	M ___ ___
2.	8000	___ E T ___
3.	360	___ A ___ A

C. Work out codes for these names and match up pairs which have the same value:

CATH   BEN   LEAH

JAN   JOE   FAYE

Challenge!

1. The names JEN and JEAN have the same code, but JEAN has an extra letter. Why? Can you find any more pairs of names like this?

2. Why is it impossible to find a name with the code 290?

Decimal four-in-a-line

- Throw a 1 to 6 dice and pick one number from the 'decimal box'.
- Multiply your two numbers together.
- If the result appears on your grid, shade it in your colour.
- Now your partner throws, chooses and colours a result.
- The winner is the first to get a line of 4 shaded numbers (horizontal, vertical or diagonal).

Decimal Box

0.1	0.2	0.3
0.4	0.5	0.6
0.7	0.8	0.9

Playing Grid

1.5	0.1	2.5	0.8	2	0.6
2.8	3.6	3.2	4.5	1.4	4.2
0.5	4.8	1.6	1	0.2	0.6
3.6	3	3.5	0.7	1.2	2.4
0.3	0.4	1.2	4	5.4	0.4
2	1.8	2.7	3	1	2.1

Decimal Multiplication and Division Maze

Sumsgalore the Wizard has to get through the mathematical maze without getting caught by the Terrible Trolls.

Calculate your way around the maze. Only correct answers will lead you to safety!

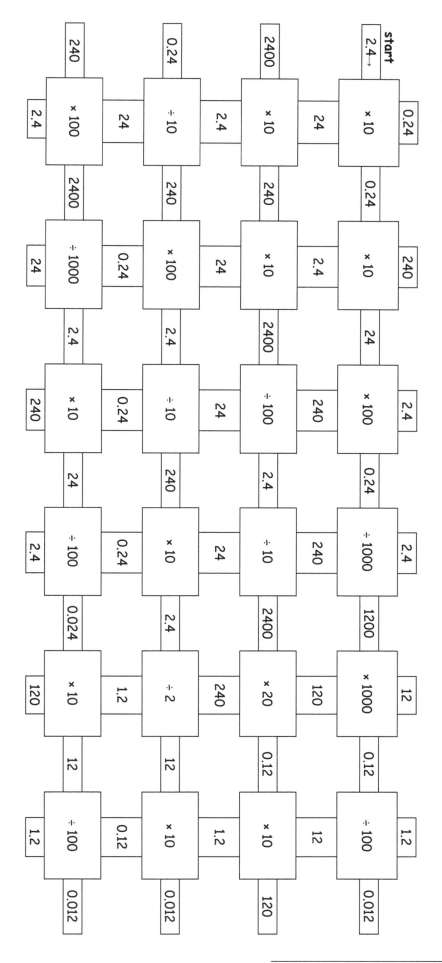

Number Machines

Use two of the following number machines to get from the input number to the output number:

| × 10 | | ÷ 10 | | + 1 |

A 9 → [×10] → [+1] → 91

B 5 → [   ] → [   ] → 1.5

C 30 → [÷10] → [+.1] → 3.1

D 20 → [   ] → [   ] → 210

E 20 → [×10] → [+1] → 201

F 60 → [÷10] → [+1] → 7

G 60 → [   ] → [   ] → 6.1

H 3 → [   ] → [   ] → 0.4

Challenge!

I 4 → [   ] → [   ] → [   ] → 4.1

J 10 → [   ] → [   ] → [   ] → 20

K 3 → [   ] → [   ] → [   ] → 1.4

That's an Order!

Put the values in the boxes in order smallest to largest. The corresponding letters should form a mathematical word.

1.
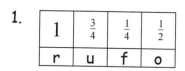

1	$\frac{3}{4}$	$\frac{1}{4}$	$\frac{1}{2}$
r	u	f	o

2.
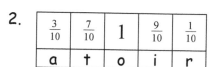

$\frac{3}{10}$	$\frac{7}{10}$	1	$\frac{9}{10}$	$\frac{1}{10}$
a	t	o	i	r

3.

$\frac{1}{2}$	$\frac{1}{3}$	1	$\frac{1}{4}$
e	r	a	a

4.
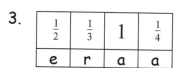

$\frac{1}{10}$	$\frac{1}{5}$	$\frac{1}{20}$	1
o	n	c	e

5.

1	$\frac{2}{3}$	$\frac{3}{4}$	$\frac{1}{2}$
e	i	m	t

6.

$\frac{2}{3}$	$\frac{5}{6}$	$\frac{1}{6}$	$\frac{1}{3}$
c	h	i	n

7.

$\frac{3}{4}$	$\frac{1}{2}$	$\frac{3}{8}$	$\frac{1}{4}$	$\frac{1}{8}$
r	e	d	r	o

8.

$\frac{3}{10}$	$\frac{1}{10}$	$\frac{19}{20}$	$\frac{1}{19}$	$\frac{9}{10}$	$\frac{11}{20}$	$\frac{1}{20}$	$\frac{1}{2}$
a	g	e	e	v	i	n	t

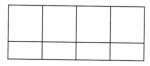

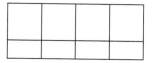
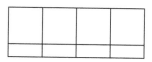

Write out the first letter of each of your words.

You should get another mathematical word!

The Maths Test

Some pupils in Miss Taken's maths class have taken a test, but she has lost some of their marks. Use the clues to fill in the missing names, marks and percentages in Miss Taken's mark book. (The test was out of 20)

Teacher : Miss Taken   Subject : Maths

Name	Mark out of 20	Percentage
Tom		
		55%
	6	
Hannah		
		65%
Ben		
	2	
Shania		
Molly		70%
		95%

- Tom got half of the test correct.

- Hannah got a quarter of the test wrong.

- Molly got as many questions wrong as Harry got right!

- Ben got $\frac{3}{5}$ of the test correct.

- Shania got one fifth of the test wrong.

- William got top marks.

- Ellie got the lowest mark.

- Callum got more marks than Harry, but less marks that Ben.

What mark and percentage did Alice get?

Four Fractions

- Throw a six-sided dice. This is the numerator of your fraction
- Choose a denominator from the box below.
- If that fraction or an equivalent fraction is on the playing grid, then shade it in your colour.
- Now the other player(s) throws the dice, chooses a denominator and colours.
- The winner is the first player to get a line of four. Lines may be horizontal, vertical or diagonal.

Denominator Box

16	9	15
12	18	10
8	6	24

Playing Grid

$\frac{1}{6}$	$\frac{2}{5}$	$\frac{5}{24}$	1	$\frac{5}{8}$	$\frac{1}{18}$
$\frac{1}{8}$	$\frac{3}{10}$	$\frac{5}{6}$	$\frac{1}{4}$	$\frac{2}{9}$	$\frac{2}{15}$
$\frac{5}{9}$	$\frac{1}{3}$	$\frac{1}{2}$	$\frac{2}{9}$	$\frac{1}{8}$	$\frac{4}{9}$
$\frac{1}{4}$	$\frac{1}{5}$	$\frac{3}{16}$	$\frac{3}{4}$	$\frac{5}{12}$	$\frac{1}{12}$
$\frac{1}{15}$	$\frac{1}{9}$	$\frac{2}{3}$	$\frac{1}{10}$	$\frac{4}{15}$	$\frac{3}{5}$
$\frac{5}{18}$	$\frac{1}{6}$	$\frac{1}{24}$	$\frac{5}{16}$	$\frac{3}{8}$	$\frac{1}{2}$

Fraction, Decimals, Percentages

Shade in the grid according to these rules:

Shade expressions equivalent to $\frac{1}{2}$ **red**

Shade expressions equivalent to $\frac{1}{4}$ **green**

Shade expressions equivalent to $\frac{1}{5}$ **yellow**

Shade expressions equivalent to $\frac{1}{10}$ **blue**

0.25	0.3	0.1	$\frac{4}{6}$	$\frac{8}{10}$	70%	$\frac{5}{10}$
0.2	80%	$\frac{3}{9}$	0.75	$\frac{2}{3}$	50%	$\frac{9}{10}$
$\frac{2}{8}$	40%	0.7	$\frac{6}{8}$	$\frac{3}{6}$	$\frac{5}{8}$	0.6
20%	$\frac{2}{6}$	90%	0.5	0.8	30%	$\frac{2}{6}$
25%	0.9	$\frac{2}{4}$	0.4	60%	$\frac{4}{10}$	10%

Write your answer as a fraction and a decimal.

Fraction Targets

$\frac{1}{4}$	$\frac{1}{2}$	$1\frac{1}{2}$	2	3

A. Use two of the above fractions to make each calculation correct:

1. [ ] + [ ] = $1\frac{3}{4}$

2. [ ] × [ ] = 3

3. [ ] - [ ] = $2\frac{3}{4}$

4. [ ] × [ ] = $1\frac{1}{2}$

5. [ ] - [ ] = $1\frac{1}{4}$

B. Use three of the above fractions to make each calculation correct:

1. [ ] + [ ] + [ ] = $2\frac{3}{4}$

2. [ ] + [ ] + [ ] = $2\frac{1}{4}$

3. [ ] + [ ] - [ ] = $3\frac{1}{2}$

4. [ ] × [ ] + [ ] = 5

Raffle Winners

The following tickets won prizes in a raffle. Use the clues to work out which prize was won by each person.

81 Hamper	**84** Bottle Wine	**135** Chocolates	**63** Day at Zoo
27 Champagne	**144** Day at Spa	**118** Movie tickets	**37** Teddy Bear
183 Cake	**71** Bowling tickets	**73** Trip to Paris	**12** Free manicure

- Tom's number is a factor of 60.

- Emma's number is an even square number.

- Pat's number is a multiple of 5.

- Shaz and Ian's numbers have a difference of 99. Shaz's number is even.

- Joe has an odd square number.

- Jill's number is a multiple of 7.

- Gem and Allie's numbers have a difference of 47. Allie's number is odd.

- Dan and Jess's numbers have a sum of 100.

- Bill and Jess's numbers have a product of 999.

The People on the Bus

The diagram on the right shows the
seating plan for a bus.

Use the clues given below to work out
who sits on which seat.

13	14	15	16	17

9	10		11	12

5	6		7	8

1	2		3	4

driver

- Max and Will sit next to each other. Their seat numbers have a
  product of 56. Will's seat number is even.

- Cath sits in front of Flo. Their seat numbers have a sum of 24.
  Cath's seat is a multiple of 5

- Dom and Ben sit on prime-numbered seats on the back row. Dom sits
  next to Flo.

- Alice sits directly behind Mo. Alice's seat number is triple Mo's.

- Jess sits on the back row on a square-numbered seat.

- Mia sits next to Dave. Their seat numbers have a product of 132.
  Mia's seat number is prime.

- Em, Pete and Lou sit on square-numbered seats. Lou's seat number is
  even. Em's seat number is a multiple of 3.

- Sam's seat number is a quarter of Dave's.

- Harry's seat number is one third of Meg's.

$6\,\overline{)16}$

$5\,\overline{)50}$

$5\,\overline{)}$

$6\,\overline{)50}$

Left...... Right......

Work out the easy question on the left and then use your answer to help you work out the more difficult question on the right.

	Left	Right
1.	$45 \div 3 = 15$	$45 \div 30 = 1.5$
2.	$2 \times 9 = 18$	$0.2 \times 0.9 = 8$
3.	$20 \times £1 = £20$	$20 \times 95p = £19$
4.	$4^2 = 16$	$40^2 = 1600$
5.	$5.1 - 3 = 4.9$	$5.1 - 2.9 = 2.2$
6.	$5 \times 4 = 20$	$4.9 \times 4 = 19.6$
7.	$£100 - £40 = £60$	$£100 - £39.85 = 60.15$
8.	$4 \times 6 = 24$	$40 \times 0.6 = 240$
9.	$2.8 \times 10 = 28$	$2.8 \times 5 = 140$
10.	10% of $50 = 5$	30% of $50 = 15$

Use the methods you have learnt to work out these:

a. $48 \div 20$ b. 0.4×0.3 c. $6.3 - 4.9$

d. 2.9×3 e. 4.6×5 f. 70% of 40

Answers

Make 10

The correct arrangement is:

```
G  F  B
A  D  I
H  E  C
```

Decimal Addition Grids

A.

+	0.7	0.8	0.1	0.6
0.3	1	1.1	0.4	0.9
0.2	0.9	1	0.3	0.8
0.5	1.2	1.3	0.6	1.1
0.9	1.6	1.7	1	1.5

B.

+	0.38	0.83	0.59	0.74
0.62	1	1.45	1.21	1.36
0.41	0.79	1.24	1	1.15
0.17	0.55	1	0.76	0.91
0.26	0.64	1.09	0.85	1

Challenge.

+	0.8	0.4	0.9
0.7	1.5	1.1	1.6
0.6	1.4	1	1.5
0.5	1.3	0.9	1.4

There is only one way of making 1 with the numbers given (0.4 + 0.6).

by also considering 0.9, it is possible to work out where the 0.4 must go.

Till Trouble

Answers are shaded.

Receipt 1

1kg apples	£1.20
1 mango	£0.99
1 pun strawberry	£0.90
total	£3.09

Receipt 2

2kg apples	£2.40
1kg oranges	£1.49
1 pun blueberry	£1.50
total	£5.39

Receipt 3

5kg potatoes	£2.50
1 lemon	£0.15
2 puns blueberry	£3.00
total	£5.65

Receipt 4

2kg potatoes	£1.00
2 mangoes	£1.98
3 lemons	£0.45
total	£3.43

Receipt 5

2kg oranges	£2.98
1 banana	£0.20
3kg apples	£3.60
total	£6.78

Receipt 6

7 bananas	£1.40
3 mangoes	£2.97
1kg pears	£1.05
total	£5.42

Receipt 7

1 bag mushrooms	£0.95
2kg pears	£2.10
3 bananas	£0.60
total	£3.65

Receipt 8

2 bag mushrooms	£1.90
½ kg apples	£0.60
5 lemons	£0.75
total	£3.25

Receipt 9

3 pun strawberry	£2.70
1½ kg apples	£1.80
2½ kg potatoes	£1.25
total	£5.75

Challenge! There are many ways of making 1. £10 and 2. £4.60. For example:

1. (20kg potatoes), (1kg pears, 1 bag mushrooms, 2 puns blueberries, 4 apples, 1 banana)

2. (2kg apples, 4kg potatoes, 1 banana), (2kg pears, 1 pun blueberry, 4 lemons, 2 bananas)

Right Height

William 0.75m	Harry 0.8m	Alice 0.91m	Tom 0.95m
Isobel 1.01m	Sam 1.08m	Yvette 1.12m	Olga 1.16m
Ursula 1.2m	Robin 1.26m	Harriet 1.27m	Emma 1.3m
Isaac 1.38m	George 1.5m	Hannah 1.55m	Tina 1.74m

The question spelt out is, 'What is your height?'

Negative Arrows

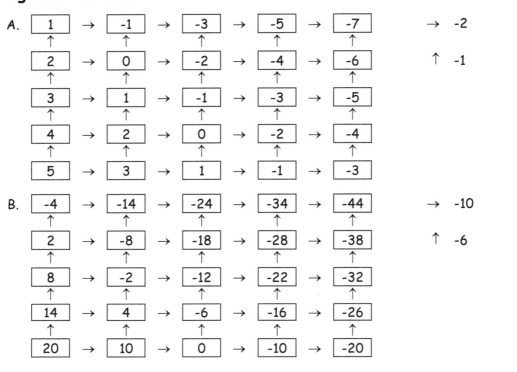

The Weather Report

The results are given in ascending order of temperature.

Helsinki (-20°C)	Calgary (-12°C)	Moscow (-10°C)	Oslo (-7°C)
Edinburgh (-5°C)	Reykjavic (-4°C)	Vienna (-3°C)	London (-2°C)
Paris (1°C)	Venice (4°C)	Tunis (15°C)	Delhi (18°C)
Cape Town (25°C)	Sydney (26°C)		

Sums and Differences for Negative Numbers

Answers are shaded.

1.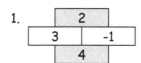

2.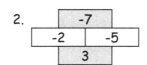

3.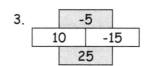

4.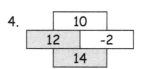

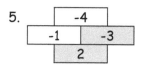 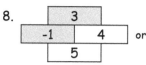 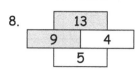 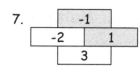

5.

	-4	
-1	-3	
	2	

6.

	-7	
4	-11	
	15	

7.

	-7	
-2	-5	
	3		or

7.

	-1	
-2	1	
	3	

8.

	3	
-1	4	
	5		or

8.

	13	
9	4	
	5	

9.

	-22	
-10	-12	
	2		or

9.

	-18	
-10	-8	
	2	

Make a Multiplication

A. 1. 3×54 = 162, 5×34 = 170, 4×35 = 140, 4×53 = 212
2. 3×45 = 135, 5×43 = 215
3. 5×34 = 170, 4×35 = 140
4. 5×43 = 215

B. 1. 23×45 = 1035, 25×43 = 1075,
2. 25×34 = 850, 35×24 = 840, 35×42 = 1470, 45×32 = 1440
3. 52×43 = 2236, 53×42 = 2226
4. 35×24 = 840

C. 1. Many answers! As long as at least one of the numbers is even, the answer will be even.
2. Several different answers, made by multiplying a number ending in 5, by an odd number.
3. 51×432 = 22032, 52×431 = 22412, 53×421 = 22313, 42×531 = 22302, 43×521 = 22403

Challenge: 13 × 245 = 3185

Make 120

2	7	11	3	2	2	14	7	2	6	5	2	13	11	2	9	2	3	2	10
2	11	3	9	13	7	3	9	12	9	7	2	2	14	3	2	2	9	13	11
15	3	20	14	3	10	20	13	5	4	3	2	7	8	4	13	3	5	4	2
2	10	3	2	11	6	12	2	3	11	13	4	9	30	15	3	2	7	13	10
9	13	2	7	2	13	9	3	2	2	2	15	14	2	11	9	5	2	2	6

The grid spells out 4 × 5 × 6 = 120.

Challenge: 1 × 120, 2 × 60, 3 × 40, 4 × 30, 5 × 24, 6 × 20, 8 × 15, 10 × 12

2 × 2 × 2 × 3 × 5 These are the **prime factors** of 120.

Number Names

A. 1. 150   2. 750   3. 216   4. 312
5. 208   6. 300   7. 504   8. 1950

B. 1. MAT   2. PETE   3. TARA

C. CATH and LEAH (480)   BEN and JAN (140)   JOE and FAYE (750)

Challenge: 1. The extra letter has value 1, which will not make any difference to the code.

2. 29 is a factor of 290 and it is a prime number, which means there are no numbers except for 1 and 29, which divide exactly into it. There is no letter in our alphabet which corresponds to the number 29.

Decimal Multiplication and Division Maze

The answers to each question are shown below. The way out is at number 240.

2.4 → 24 → 240 → 2400 → 24 → 2.4 → 240 → 24 → 2400 → 2.4 → 24 → 0.24 → 2.4 → 1.2 →
12 → 0.12 → 1.2 → 12 → 0.12 → 120 → 2400 → 240 → 0.24 → 24 → 240

Number Machines

Questions D, E and F, G can be used to demonstrate how order matters.

A	9	→	×10	→	+1	→	91		E	20	→	×10	→	+1	→	201
B	5	→	÷10	→	+1	→	1.5		F	60	→	÷10	→	+1	→	7
C	30	→	+1	→	÷10	→	3.1		G	60	→	+1	→	÷10	→	6.1
D	20	→	+1	→	×10	→	210		H	3	→	+1	→	÷10	→	0.4

Challenge:

I	4	→	×10	→	+1	→	÷10	→	4.1
J	10	→	÷10	→	+1	→	×10	→	20
K	3	→	+1	→	÷10	→	+1	→	1.4

That's an Order!

1. | $\frac{1}{4}$ | $\frac{1}{2}$ | $\frac{3}{4}$ | 1 |
   | f | o | u | r |

2. | $\frac{1}{10}$ | $\frac{3}{10}$ | $\frac{7}{10}$ | $\frac{9}{10}$ | 1 |
   | r | a | t | i | o |

3. | $\frac{1}{4}$ | $\frac{1}{3}$ | $\frac{1}{2}$ | 1 |
   | a | r | e | a |

4. | $\frac{1}{20}$ | $\frac{1}{10}$ | $\frac{1}{5}$ | 1 |
   | c | o | n | e |

5. | $\frac{1}{2}$ | $\frac{2}{3}$ | $\frac{3}{4}$ | 1 |
   | t | i | m | e |

6. | $\frac{1}{6}$ | $\frac{1}{3}$ | $\frac{2}{3}$ | $\frac{5}{6}$ |
   | i | n | c | h |

7. | $\frac{1}{8}$ | $\frac{1}{4}$ | $\frac{3}{8}$ | $\frac{1}{2}$ | $\frac{3}{4}$ |
   | o | r | d | e | r |

8. | $\frac{1}{20}$ | $\frac{1}{19}$ | $\frac{1}{10}$ | $\frac{3}{10}$ | $\frac{1}{2}$ | $\frac{11}{20}$ | $\frac{9}{10}$ | $\frac{19}{20}$ |
   | n | e | g | a | t | i | v | e |

The first letter of each of the words spells 'fraction'.

The Maths Test

Tom 10/20, 50%   Callum 11/20, 55%   Harry 6/20, 30%

Hannah 15/20, 75%   Alice 13/20, 65%   Ben 12/20, 60%

Ellie 2/20, 10%   Shania 16/20, 80%   Molly 14/20, 70%

William 19/20, 95%   (The only score remaining is 65%, which must be Alice's)

Fractions Decimals and Percentages

0.25	0.3	0.1	$\frac{4}{6}$	$\frac{8}{10}$	70%	$\frac{5}{10}$
0.2	80%	$\frac{3}{9}$	0.75	$\frac{2}{3}$	50%	$\frac{9}{10}$
$\frac{2}{8}$	40%	0.7	$\frac{6}{8}$	$\frac{3}{6}$	$\frac{5}{8}$	0.6
20%	$\frac{2}{6}$	90%	0.5	0.8	30%	$\frac{2}{6}$
25%	0.9	$\frac{2}{4}$	0.4	60%	$\frac{4}{10}$	10%

The '1' is alternately green and yellow. The diagonal line of the % sign is red and the dots are blue.

So the answer is 1%, which is $\frac{1}{100}$ as a fraction and 0.01 as a decimal.

Fraction Targets

For numbers which are added or multiplied, the order does not matter.

A. 1. $1\frac{1}{2} + \frac{1}{4}$ 2. $2 \times 1\frac{1}{2}$ 3. $3 - \frac{1}{4}$ 4. $3 \times \frac{1}{2}$ 5. $1\frac{1}{2} - \frac{1}{4}$

B. 1. $2 + \frac{1}{2} + \frac{1}{4}$ 2. $1\frac{1}{2} + \frac{1}{4} + \frac{1}{2}$ 3. $2 + 3 - 1\frac{1}{2}$ 4. $2 \times 1\frac{1}{2} + 2$

Raffle Winners

Joe – hamper	Shaz – wine	Pat – chocolates	Jill – day at zoo
Jess – champagne	Emma – day at spa	Gem – movie tickets	Bill – teddy bear
Ian – cake	Allie – bowling	Dan – trip to Paris	Tom - manicure

The People on the Bus

1	Pete	2	Mo	3	Sam	4	Lou
5	Harry	6	Alice	7	Max	8	Will
9	Em	10	Cath	11	Mia	12	Dave
13	Dom	14	Flo	15	Meg	16	Jess
17	Ben						

Left......   Right......

This activity practices a really important skill: Using a known answer to help you work out a more difficult calculation. I would encourage plenty of class discussion and work in pairs or groups, to help pupils become aware of the different methods and 'tricks', which can be used.

1.	$45 \div 3 = 15$	$45 \div 30 = 1.5$	45 is being divided by a number 10× greater, so the answer will be 10× smaller
2.	$2 \times 9 = 18$	$0.2 \times 0.9 = 0.18$	Each value is 10× less so that answer will be 100× less
3.	$20 \times £1 = £20$	$20 \times 95p = £19$	95p is 5p less than £1, so the answer will be 20× 5p less than £20.
4.	$4^2 = 16$	$40^2 = 1600$	40 × 40 is 100× greater than 4 × 4
5.	$5.1 - 3 = 2.1$	$5.1 - 2.9 = 2.2$	0.1 less is being subtracted, so the answer will be 0.1 more.
6.	$5 \times 4 = 20$	$4.9 \times 4 = 19.6$	4.9 is 0.1 less than 5, so the answer will be 4 × 0.1 less
7.	$£100 - £40 = £60$	$£100 - £39.85 = £60.15$	£39.85 is 15p less than £40, so the answer will be 15p more.
8.	$4 \times 6 = 24$	$40 \times 0.6 = 24$	4 has been multiplied by 10, 6 has been divided by 10. These operations cancel each other out so answer remains the same.
9.	$2.8 \times 10 = 28$	$2.8 \times 5 = 14$	Answer will be half, as 5 is half of 10.
10.	10% of 50 = 5	30% of 50 = 15	30% = 3 × 10%, so the answer will be 3× greater.

	Answer	Easy calculation to be used
a.	2.4	$48 \div 10$
b.	0.12	4×3
c.	1.4	$6.3 - 5$
d.	8.7	3×3
e.	23	4.6×10
f.	28	10% of 40

Lightning Source UK Ltd.
Milton Keynes UK
UKHW05f1831300818
328061UK00003B/12/P